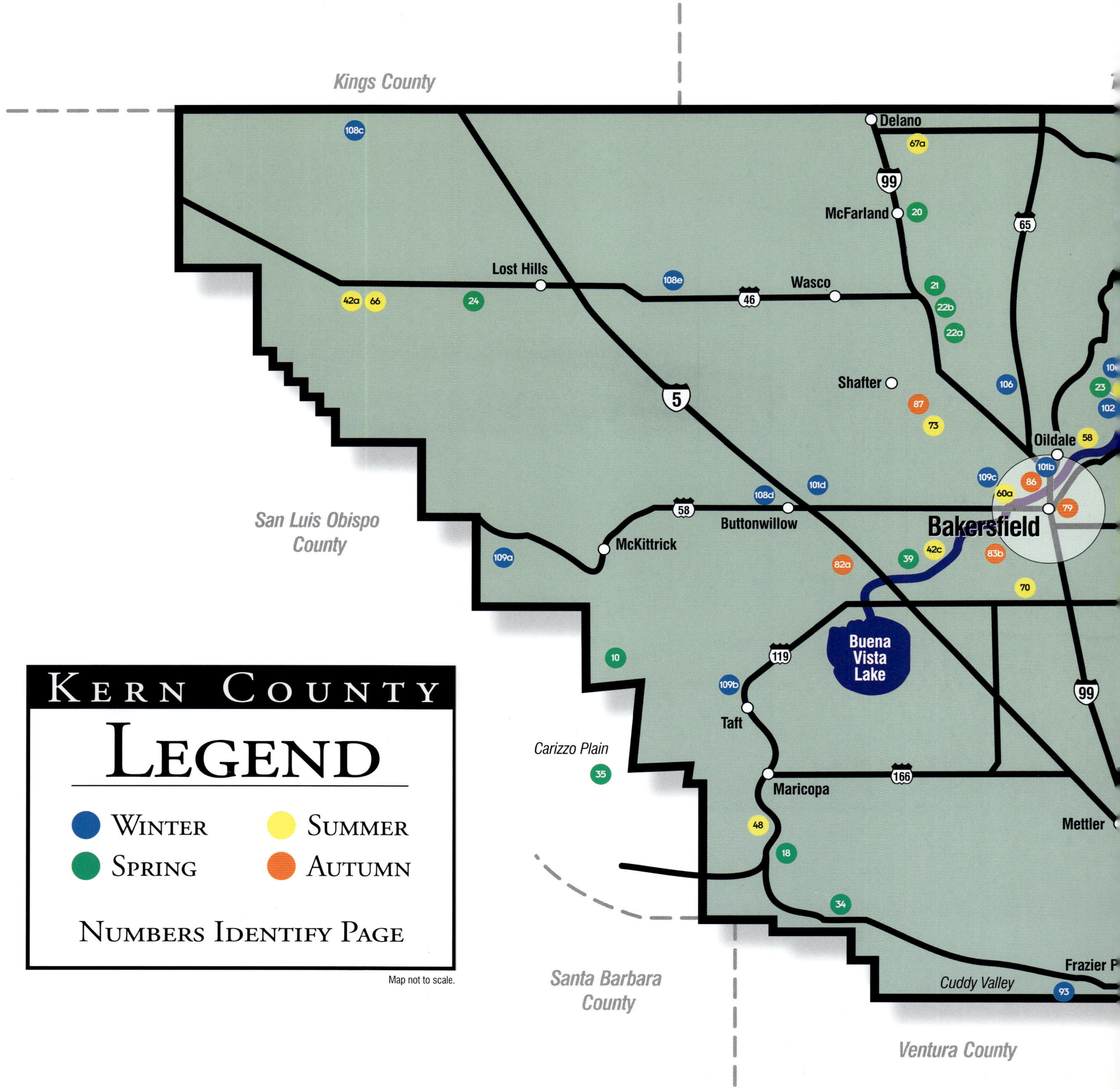

Map not to scale.

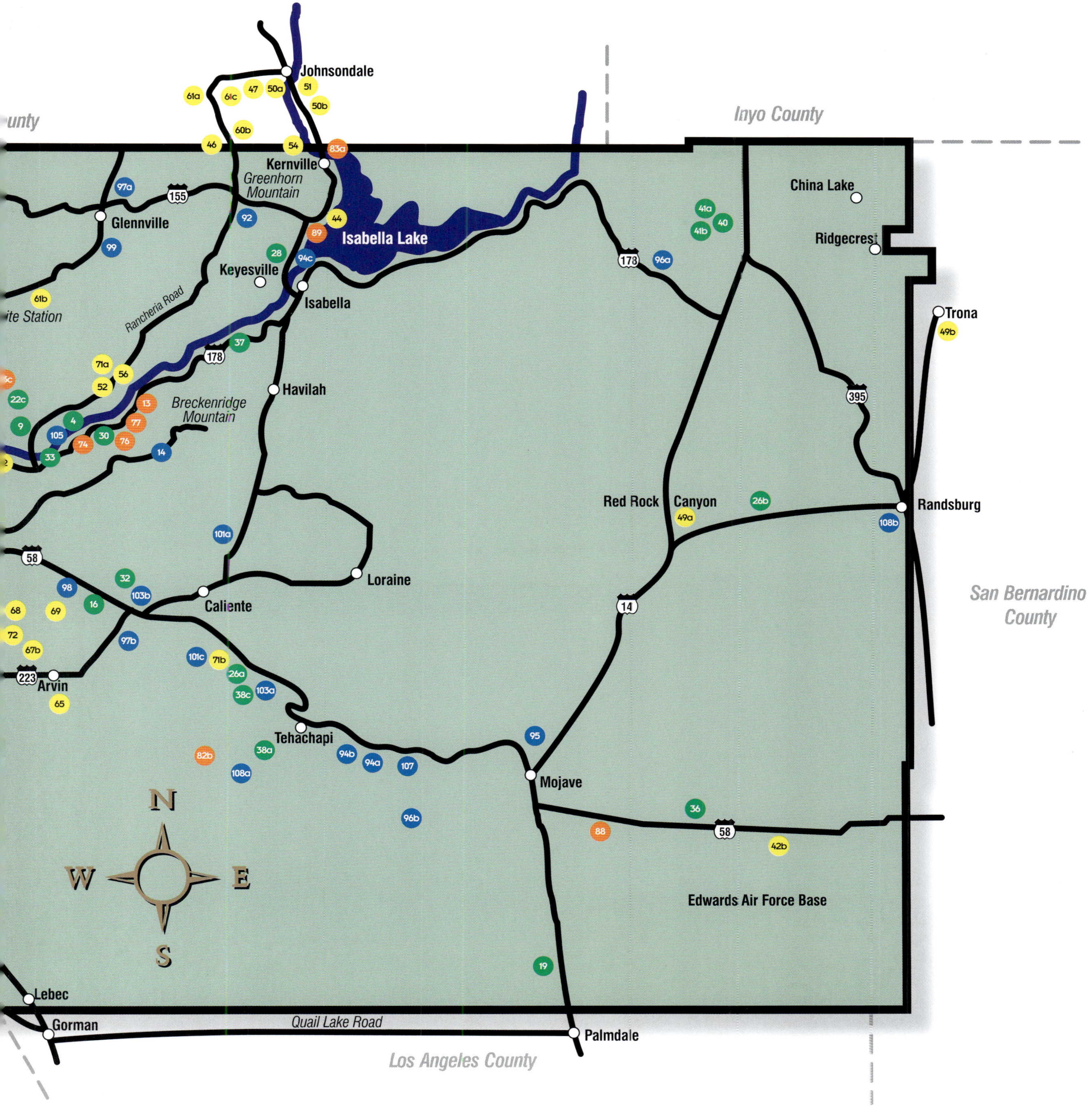

Johnsondale
Inyo County
Kernville
Greenhorn Mountain
Glennville
Isabella Lake
Keyesville
Isabella
Rancheria Road
China Lake
Ridgecrest
Trona
Havilah
Breckenridge Mountain
Red Rock Canyon
Randsburg
Loraine
Caliente
San Bernardino County
Arvin
Tehachapi
Mojave
Edwards Air Force Base
N
W
E
S
Lebec
Gorman
Quail Lake Road
Palmdale
Los Angeles County

Rancheria Road

Spring poppies in the foothills create one of those perfect moments.

BUENA VISTA II

KERN COUNTY LANDSCAPES

Photography and Text by
Gregory Iger

Edited by
Jill Egland

Forward by
Herb Benham

211 H Street, Bakersfield, California 93304

(805) 327-2768

Printed in Hong Kong through Bolton Associates, San Raphael, California

Designed by Committee

Layout and Map Art by Tim Cairns

Project Development by Jill Egland

First Printing

ISBN 0-9660939-0-9 (clothbound)

ISBN 0-9660939-1-7 (paperback)

Publication of this book would not have been possible without the generous support of the following individuals and corporations:

Mr. and Mrs. Rayburn S. Dezember
Michael and Marci Tivnon
Robert E. McCarthy, III; Lightspeed Net
Borton, Petrini & Conron
Lortz Manufacturing; Charles W. Lortz, Jr.
The George Nickel Family
Golden Empire Concrete
The Stinson Family
KGET - TV 17

Our thanks also to:

ARCO Western Energy
Kern Recreation Camp
Three Way Chevrolet Company
Linda and Richard Sullenger
Holly and Bill Lazzerini
Coldwell Banker Preferred, Realtors®
Katherine C. Iger
Sunridge Nursery; Glen and Terrie Stoller
Steven Lewis; Petro Chem Environmental Services
Rain for Rent Irrigation Systems
Kern Schools Federal Credit Union

To my wife, Deborah, who always had love and dinner waiting,
no matter how late that sunset.

To Sunday and Chelsea, my darling daughters.

To my loyal customers, who have made it all possible.

To Teri, for keeping a watchful eye on the business while I produced this book.

To Jill, for keeping me from looking foolish.

To these special people:
Tim Cairns; Joanne Bolton; Dodo Nickel; Linda Sullenger;
Michael, Cindy, Jamie and Charlotte at Rosedale Photo Lab;
Wood and Mary at Specialized Photo Graphics; the Kern County Water Agency;
the Bureau of Land Management; and the Ridgecrest Convention and Visitors' Bureau.

To Charlie Brannen, Clay Rutledge, Bruce Lochrie and Jerry Sparling for keeping me company on road trips.

And finally, to the members of the Kern River Parkway Foundation,
who are bringing a long-held dream of our community into reality.

Rio Bravo Ranch
Terraced almond trees are seen in full bloom below the foothills.

Poppy Motif
An aerial view of a hillside of poppies near Taft resembles brushstrokes on an artist's canvas.

FORWARD

I don't know how many times I've been somewhere — halfway up Breckenridge threading my way through a sea of gold grass, White Wolf Grade in the spring when it's in wild flower heaven, or the bend of the Kern River on a moonlit morning — and wished I'd had a camera.

It's almost enough to experience it, to write about it, but to be armed at the critical moment with a 35mm, that would be chopped pecans on a Dewar's Black and White.

While I've been in a state of perpetual longing, Greg Iger has been doing it. Snapping pictures at odd times, early times, all times. Doing what most of us here have wanted to do as much out of spite as pride; that is, show the world just how beautiful this corner of the San Joaquin Valley is.

Most of us weren't just left here by the turkey buzzards on a sweep northward. We chose to leave here and we chose to return. We threaten to leave if it gets too crowded, but we're not going anywhere because this country has left its taste as indelible as juice from a Flame Seedless.

Greg Iger is a clever fellow. I suppose you must be to be a photographer, but especially a photographer documenting season, splash and color in this hot, dry part of the valley. It is one thing to live at the ocean and have the seals bouncing up and down on rocks, or in the mountains and have Half Dome as the backdrop for every photograph you take.

But it's quite another to have barbed wire fences, bare stretches that look like Mars and great expanses of flat land that make one feel as insignificant as a flea on a mountain lion (yes, we have those, too).

This is not landscape, life or climate for the impatient, the particular, the sluggish, or the soft. When the heat comes in June, it's not going anywhere for a couple months. It doesn't do any good to jump up and down and demand your rights. This is your town. This is the life you have chosen.

Most of us who call this home are glad to do so. We sense we have something here. Something as important, as real and spectacular, as any plunging North Coast landscape.

This is a hardy, beautiful, varied place, but you have to show up to see it. Iger has done that. Show up. Again and again.

And for those who think Kern County is just six blessed off ramps before you get to where you really want to go, may I suggest thumbing though this book. You shouldn't be surprised, but you will. It's almost as good as living here.

Herb Benham, Bakersfield, 1997

Kern County

The year was 1772. Spanish troops trekked through the narrow, twisting ravines of an unfamiliar mountain trail. After many days, the band came upon a broad valley stretching endlessly northward. "¡*Buena Vista!*" declared their commander, Don Pedro Fages.

Another 100 years would pass before the region would officially be known by anything other than Fages' understatement. History bestowed that honor to the memory of Edward M. Kern, chief artist and topographer to explorer John C. Fremont.

Encompassing a horseshoe of mountain ranges at the southern end of the San Joaquin Valley, Kern County covers 8,172 square miles of perhaps the most diverse landscape in the country. Its western border is marked by the Temblor Range; within it, the San Andreas Fault. Wells scattered over fields and foothills attest to the region's richness in oil. A mosaic of nature sanctuaries are also here: Bitter Creek, Carrizo Plain, Wind Wolves, Tule Elk.

The Tehachapi Mountains mark the southern border. I-5 enters the range by traversing up the Grapevine Canyon, then passing historic Fort Tejon and crossing through Tejon Ranch. Just outside the mountain community of Frazier Park stands Mount Pinos. Kern's highest elevation is on its north slope.

The high desert spans the entire eastern border. Highway 58 winds through the Tehachapis, then crosses over the great Mojave. Several miles north, Highway 178 follows the Kern Canyon up into the rugged magnificence of the southern Sierra Nevada Mountains, then drops into the arid winds of the Indian Wells Valley.

To the north extends the San Joaquin Valley, as awesome today as when Fages first gazed down upon it over 200 years ago. Highway 99 links together the dozens of small farming communities that now dot the landscape. Delano, Kern County's northern-most town, marks the start of Highway 155, which connects the Central Valley to the Sequoia National Forest. The frontier towns of Glennville and Kernville, and the mountain community of Alta Sierra provide gateways into the wilderness of the Sierra Nevada.

Running through the county is the Kern River. Formed by the watershed of the high Sierra, the river begins its 126-mile journey at the western slope of Mount Whitney. It cascades down the Kern Canyon to the valley floor, where it passes through Bakersfield, Kern's largest city. The river is siphoned into a network of canals and finally terminates at Buena Vista Lake.

> I WALK IN BEAUTY PAST MEADOW AND
> MOUNTAIN AND TARN, GATHERING THE SEEDS OF
> FAITH, FROM ALL THE WILD MIRACLES OF MY
> PRISTINE WORLD.
>
> *Ardis Manly Walker*

Kern Canyon

River willows light up the canyon in late fall.

Breckenridge
Storm clouds race across the valley floor.

The Seasons

Bear Mountain, off Highway 58
An early spring view of green grass and granite.

Spring

From out of the ice, fog and chilling winds of winter, the rebirth begins. Snow melt and runoff feed life-giving nutrients to the vegetation of the San Joaquin Valley. As the sun warms the valley's fertile soil, life renews itself: first, with fresh green buds on the trees; next, with the resurgence of grasses and wildflowers; and then, with the blossoming of agricultural crops. Spring nurtures our bodies and sustains our souls.

Such narratives of the genesis of life have been tirelessly employed by poets and journalists. But words are meaningless for the unassuming photographer tromping through a muddy bog to find the first flower of the season.

Spring is a feeling, a color, a cool breeze. The photographer's quest: to capture the feeling and share it with those who may identify, marvel or simply enjoy the view.

In Kern County, the transition from winter to spring is obscure. For most of us, the end of the fog season marks spring's true birth. Landscapes, their depths lost in the flat light of winter, become three dimensional again. As the sun spreads its illuminating rays, shapes take on new colors. Colors, in turn, unfold in layers to reveal new contours.

Spring means storms, and with these storms come incredible skies. Puffy white clouds against an intense blue become the ceiling to a panorama of mountain ranges.

"When I was a kid, I could see the Grapevine from my front porch," claim most of us over thirty. The facts? Who knows. It's true that the mountains surround us on three sides. It's also true that between winter's fog and summer's haze, it's easy to forget from one spring to the next just how close those mountains really are.

Spring, all by itself, creates an endless palette for the photographer. Close your eyes, point your camera in any direction ... and shoot.

CERRO NOROESTE ROAD
Clouds reflect on an irrigation pond.

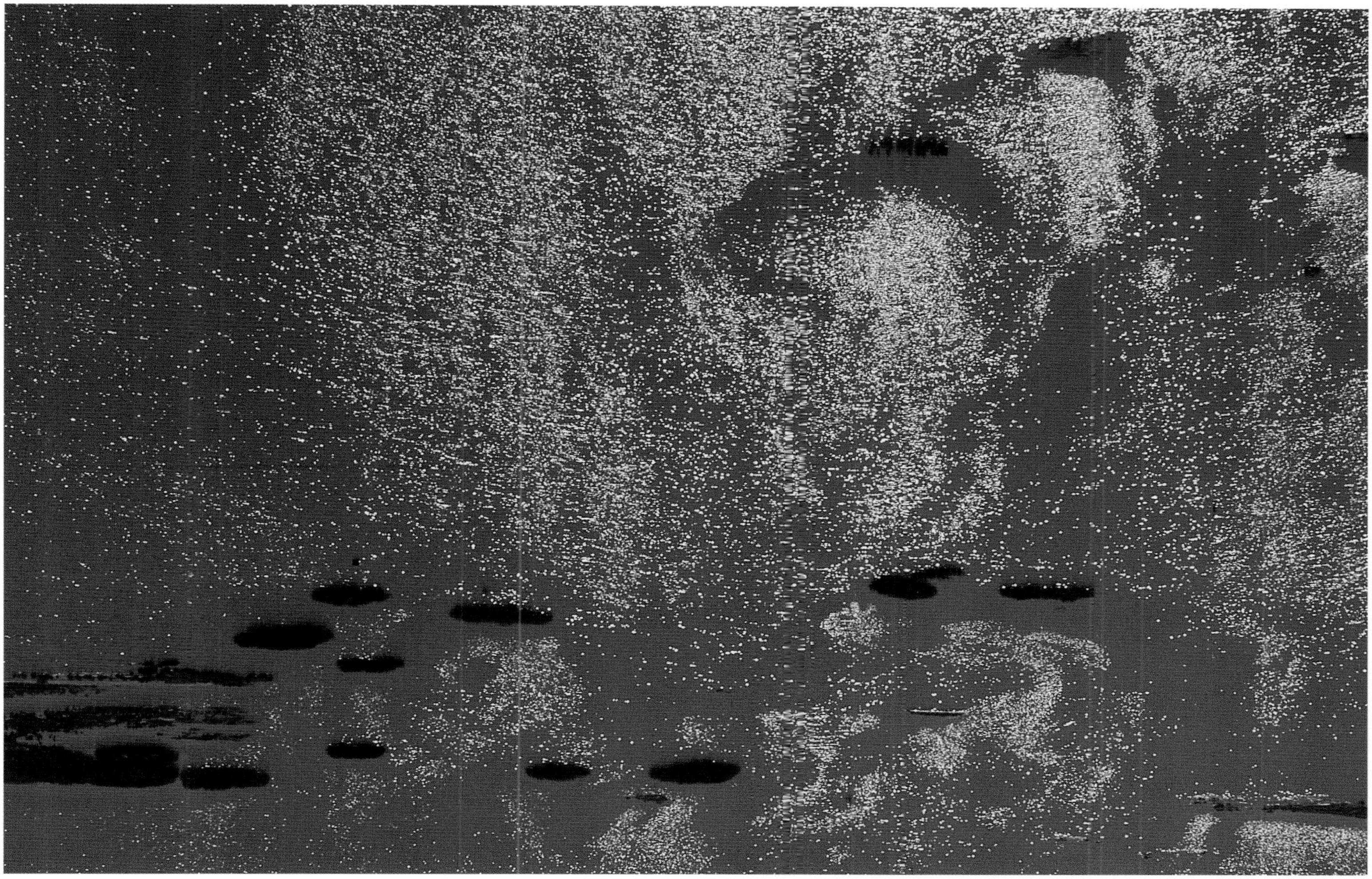

NEAR ROSAMOND
An aerial shot of the sun’s reflection in Piute Ponds.

Almond Blossoms, Near McFarland

For a few short weeks in March, the valley floor is dominated by the delicate, signaling spring is about to begin.

McFarland
A roadrunner seeks refuge in a blossoming almond tree.

Clockwise from top left:

a. Peach and plum blossoms

b. Ornamental peach blossoms

c. Apricot trees in bloom, Kern Canyon in the background

KERN RIVER
The sky lights up with the last rays of the sun.

Cumulus clouds, near Blackwell's Corner

The important thing to me about clouds, photographically, is that they break up a bald sky. I love storm chasing, though. I'll drive up Breckenridge Mountain where it's possible to watch as the storm progresses across the valley floor. Sometimes it's a race; at other times, a slow stroll. Always it's a bob and weave, a mix and remix of blues and blacks, a drama of colors and shapes. And eventually, the sun peeks through, changing the entire scene, creating a cinematic invitation to heaven.

Clockwise from top left: a. Cumulus lenticulus at sunset   b. Cumulus thunderhead over the Kern Canyon   c. Cumulus Christus   d. Layers of fracto-cumulus clouds

a. Baby blue-eyes

b. Desert dandelion

From the first filaree of February to the last sunflower of September, Kern County is famous for its wild flowers. The cycle begins on the valley floor, where blossoms grace open fields, rise along roadsides and soften abandoned lots. Then suddenly, they burst into bloom and saturate the foothills.

In abundant years, hillsides look virtually painted with splashes of color. Gradually, wildflowers appear at higher and higher elevations until finally the mountain meadows are filled with fragrance and adorned with nature's tiny masterpieces.

GRAPEVINE FOOTHILLS
Spring rains produce a sea of poppies, lupines and owl's clover.

Goldfields, Near Keyesville
This tiny yellow flower is prolific enough to cover miles of hillsides.

Clockwise from top left:
a. Chick lupine
b. White lupine
c. Mojave aster

Kern Canyon Wall

They say the wildflowers that bloom following a brush fire are the most brilliant and abundant of all. These blossoms saturate a canyon wall that nine months earlier was decimated by fire.

One early spring day in 1984, I remember driving up Rancheria Road looking for wildflower shots. I wasn't having much success. Just as I was thinking of turning back, I came around a bend in the road and was hit with the most amazing scene. There before me was the entire south side of a group of hills lit in an intense tangerine.

I slowly pulled over and sat in my car, speechless. Poppies do this to a person.

There are many stories about how the poppy came to be California's state flower. I personally believe the decision was made on a day in early March. The committee took a break, stepped outside, and was so overwhelmed by the splash of orange brilliance in the fields surrounding them that they forgot all about the competition.

Clockwise from top left:

a. Inside a poppy

b. Poppy's best friend, blue lupine

c. Poppy's eye view

Caliente Hills
Green grasses cover the landscape.

Kern River, at Rio Bravo Ranch

Padre Francisco Garces came upon the river in 1776 and named it Rio de San Felipe. *Not a swimmer, he was bodily ferried across by four Yokuts. "I took the opportunity to bathe at my pleasure," he later wrote.*

Cerro-Noroeste Road

Eroded sandstone reigns over this rarely traveled back country. San Andreas fault is visible in the background.

The Carrizo Plain

A long drive, but worth it — especially in spring! Goldfields and owl's clover seem to stretch the length of the plain.

Mojave Desert

a. Joshua and goldfields are illuminated after a rare desert rain. Inset: b. Joshua blossom

Democrat Hot Springs
California buckeye trees in blossom cover the western slopes of the southern Sierra.

a. Oaks, Tehachapi

b. Creek, Fort Tejon

c. Meadow, Keene Ranch

Aerial, Stockdale
A water spreading pond recharges valuable aquifers.

Short Canyon

Miniature sand dunes welcome you to Short Canyon. Two peaks, Owens and Jenkins, loom in the background.

a. METAMORPHIC ROCK, SHORT CANYON
Stark boulders and forgotten terrain are reminiscent of the old westerns.

Inset: b. NEAR RIDGECREST
Cholla cactus display their treacherous needles in the sunlight.

a. LOST HILLS HORIZON
Looking west after sunset, the hills of the Temblor range seem to imitate each other.

b. BORON
Dry lake bed

c. STOCKDALE
"Big ball" sunset through cottonwoods.

SUMMER

As the summer sun reaches the Sierra and the snow melt accelerates, waterways fill to their capacity. Creeks cascade over rocky edifices, lakes overflow, and the Kern River becomes a raging torrent. The river is an awesome spectacle when powering its way down the canyon, a force too grand to be reckoned with.

Kern County is famous for its summer. The standard quip is: "We have four seasons. There's one month each of fall, winter and spring … and nine months of summer!" The official term for it is *semi-arid*. Whatever. It translates into a nine month stretch of balmy nights, barbecues, moonlit swims and convertibles.

It's true, you can't ignore the heat, nor do we want to. Kern County *is* agriculture, and agriculture is the product of the intense heat of summer. Kern County blows away the world's notion of farming with its abundance, its ability to produce three crops in one year.

The beauty of this situation is not only financial, it's artistic as well. The variety of the harvest, the diversity of colors and shapes, bestow an unexpected richness of subject matter.

For the photographer, summer is a time of full-blown color. The river is royal blue, the sun sets in brilliant orange. Trees, having reached the peak of their cycle, are now lush canopies of green. Foothills are set in motion by golden grasses rippling in the hot wind.

The haze of the summer sky creates an illusion of distance. From the valley, the surrounding mountains soften and fade into the background, creating layers of subtle color, separating one elevation from another.

It's a whole different world in the mountains. It can be 110° F. on the valley floor, but in less than an hour you can be laying on your back in a lush green meadow, looking up at the bluest sky you've ever seen! Aspens and cottonwoods flicker as they catch the cool breezes. High country meadows still harbor many varieties of wild flowers. Creeks and streams taunt you to cast a line.

Lake Isabella

Spring and summer snow melts usually fill the lake to capacity and immerse the incredibly hearty cottonwood and willow trees.

Fort Tejon
A canopy of green is formed by this grove of oaks, thought to be the oldest in Kern County.

Portuguese Meadow
A hollowed out ponderosa pine shelters young corn lilies.

Frog Meadow

Ponderosa pine and marsh grasses make this southern Sierra meadow a great place to cool off in midsummer.

San Emigdio Range

Erosion arroyos contrast with the dry grasses in early morning sunlight.

a. Red Rock Canyon State Park
A dramatic component of the high desert, the Red Rock Canyon is a fantastic example of the power of wind and erosion — and it's also a popular movie set.

Inset: b. Trona Pinnacles
Giant tufa towers rise surrealistically out of the desert floor.

a. ROCKY EDIFICE

An upper canyon wall stair-steps down to Johnsondale Bridge.

Inset: b. NEAR LIMESTONE CAMPGROUND

An underground spring seeps through the rock, producing a mysterious, algae-covered, weeping wall.

South Creek Falls

The 100-foot drop marks the end of South Creek's journey to the Kern River. The close-up action is frozen by a fast shutter speed of 1/500 sec. at f9.5.

Mid-way, Kern River
Deep shade in the canyon provides a perfect opportunity for a time exposure: 4 sec. at f32, with a polarizing filter.

The Kern River is a paradox. It's the life blood of the region — there'd be little in the way of agriculture without it. It's a community landmark — the place to go when temperatures soar into the 100's. It's a thing of complex beauty and an ever-changing nature show. It's also one of the most dangerous bodies of water in the country, dropping in elevation faster than any river west of the Mississippi.

For me, it's been an exceptionally inspiring photographic subject over the years. I never tire of its ever-changing face: tumbling rapids, swirling currents and calm reflections of blue, green, red and orange. It twists, turns and winds its way through 120 miles of canyons, meadows and rocky cascades. When my creativity needs recharging, I can jump into my car and in 20 minutes be in the canyon, looking upon whichever face the Kern has chosen to wear that day.

Near Corral Creek Campground
Just north of Kernville the canyon opens up, letting the sky's reflection paint the river a brilliant shade of blue.

The Many Faces of the Kern River

The Kern River

If I could show you how I feel about the Kern River, this picture would say it all.

Iger Overlook
A late summer sunset reflects on the Shadow Hills, near Gordon's Ferry.

Floating the Kern:

Tips on a Safe Encounter

- If you're not a swimmer, stay away from the river.
- Use a tube! In 40 years of river floating experience, I remain committed to the simple car tire inner tube. It's the most fun, the safest, and the most maneuverable floating device.
- Never enter the river while under the influence of drugs or alcohol.
- Don't try to swim in Levi's. They get heavy when they're wet, and they'll pull you down!
- In general, travel feet first to push off rocks or branches, and stay in the middle.
- Always float with a buddy, but don't tie tubes together … and never tie yourself, your child or a pet to a tube. Children should always wear a life jacket.
- Respect the power of the current. Don't try to swim against it or across it.
- To get out of the river, relax and float downstream at an angle toward an area without bushes or tree limbs.

Clockwise from top left:
a. Snow plant
b. Jimsonweed
c. Sunflowers

a. Water Hyacinths

Treasure to one, nemesis to another. While beautiful in bloom, the floating plant chokes weirs and inlets.

b. Portuguese Pass

Scarlet penstemon light up the pass with their red-orange glow, and provide a welcomed break from the dusty back roads of the Greenhorn Mountains.

Clockwise from top left:

a. POISON MEADOW
Corn lily

b POZO FLAT
Yucca in bloom

c. NEAR TYLER MEADOW
Fireweed

Near Lake Ming
Wild oats dance under the threatening sky of a summer storm.

Hart Park
They say a thousand diamond rings lay at the bottom of the lake at Hart Park.

ARVIN
Sprinkler mist over a carrot field casts a soft rainbow.

Agriculture is Kern County. Start with rich, loamy soil. Add an abundant water supply from the Kern River, a series of well-managed aquifers, and one of the most elaborate canal systems in the US. Sprinkle in 250 sunny days — 100 of which average over 90° F. — and *voila!* Behold a growing season that encompasses three quarters of the year and produces as much as three crops from the same acreage.

The impact such bounty has on our economy is obvious. The impact it has on the artist sometimes needs to be discovered.

In the late 60's, I worked for United Press International out of the Los Angeles bureau. I was sent back to Kern County to produce an even-handed story of Cesar Chavez, the grape workers' strike and the farmers' point of view.

I was side tracked by the Thompson Seedless grape. Completely intrigued by their beauty, I spent the entire day with my camera in the vineyards, forgetting the politics that had brought me there. This was my first realization that the crops grown in our valley have more than an economic significance.

Agriculture is a source of creative art: The stark white of cotton against a deep blue sky. Morning dew clinging, pearl-like, to a cluster of Ribier grapes. Sprinkler mist rainbows arched over a forest of carrot tops. Mottled patterns of red and orange made by sunlight on a peach. The beauty is exposed in countless ways.

Lost Hills Vineyard
Golden hills and grapevines border the west side of the valley along Highway 46.

Above: a. **DELANO**
Kern's famous table grape harvest features the Dawn Seedless, offspring of the popular Thompson Seedless.

Right: b. **NEAR WEEDPATCH**
A more recent development is the claret colored Flame Seedless, pioneered by John Kavacavich. Tastes like candy on the vine!

LAMONT

Row crops are a significant valley feature. Bell peppers of every type and color are abundant.

DiGiorgio

Early summer cotton cultivation produces an October harvest.

Pumpkin Center

Golden grains of wheat sway gently in semi-tropic breezes.

a. KEENE RANCH
Sheep graze in the Croston alluvial fan.

b. RANCHERIA ROAD
Cattle stop their grazing while their portraits are taken. Red individual history tags are stapled to their ears.

Near Lamont

Varieties of organically grown lettuce — finally, art and health unite!

AERIAL, CALLOWAY CANAL
Blue canals cut across green alfalfa fields producing linear images of contrasting colors and shapes.

Kern Canyon Road
Virginia creeper grows on the canyon wall. Green in summer, this vine goes through a succession of brilliant color changes in early fall.

AUTUMN

Autumn creeps into Kern County, as 100° F. days increasingly give way to 40° F. nights. You may not even know summer has ended until you smell the Thanksgiving turkey!

Unlike the burst of brilliance associated with a New England September, autumn colors in Kern evolve gradually. The season usually peaks in mid-November, and often sustains pockets of orange and yellow radiance well beyond Christmas.

From the perspective of the photographer, autumn is an exhibition. To enter the gallery, you must travel to the higher elevations. There, single aspen, sycamore and cottonwood trees display a brilliant contrast to the surrounding deep greens of the sugar pines and Douglas firs. The sky is clear, the air is crisp, and the days are still warm enough to travel around in shirt sleeves.

Later in the season, the exhibition space grows to include the foothills and valley floor. Kern Canyon is lined with yellow river willows, which stand in sharp distinction to the steel gray of the granite and the deep-pool blackness of the quiet Kern River.

In the cities and towns of the valley, most of the season's hues are found on domesticated trees, many over 100 years old, which were undoubtedly cultivated by transplanted New Englanders homesick for East Coast autumns. There are brilliant reds amongst the Chinese pistachios and fruit trees. Willows and cottonwoods produce such a bright shade of yellow, they'll hurt your eyes.

At the center of our gallery is the liquidambar (sweet gum). Each leaf moves at its own unique pace through the autumn color spectrum, resulting in every tree being a virtual rainbow of greens, golds, oranges and reds.

Kern Canyon
River willows reflect on calm water.

Kern Canyon
The river is reduced to its lowest level in late autumn. Willows and sycamores add interest.

Hart Park

Chinese pistache trees dominate the autumn color in the park.

Oleander Avenue
A mature Chinese pistache brightens up the neighborhood.

Clockwise from top left:
a. Fruitless mulberry
b. Ornamental flowering pear
c. Ginko
d. Sycamore

Yes, Kern County abounds with fall color. As our forests are made up primarily of oaks and evergreens, the most consistently spectacular color is seen within the city limits.

Wander up into the mountains, though, and the vibrancy of coloration displayed by the aspens, willows and sycamores might even impress a New Englander. In the valley and along the river, cottonwoods, sycamores and willows turn lovely shades of amber and yellow.

When I look for autumn color, I'm drawn to Hart Park, where years ago, some forward-thinking community leader had the wherewithal to plant hundreds of beautiful trees, including two of my favorites — the showy liquidambar and Chinese pistache.

Clockwise from top left: a. Crape myrtle b. Liquidambar c. Scarlet oak

Above: a. TUPMAN
Nineteenth century cattle baron Henry Miller donated the land that today serves as the Tule Elk State Reserve.

Left: b. STALLION SPRINGS
Grazing in the dry brush, a mule deer keeps a watchful eye on golfers.

Clockwise from top left:

a. KERNVILLE
The great blue heron reside all along the Kern River. They create quite a spectacle taking off.

b. STOCKDALE
Ibis are caught in flight with a 500mm lens, 1/500 sec., at f8.

c. HART PARK
A snowy egret fishes in a marshy tributary at the park.

When the sun nears the horizon and cuts through the earth's atmosphere, we're provided with a magnificent light show. In smoggy summer and foggy winter, the setting sun becomes a big orange ball that dips into the horizon — a dramatic, yet predictable event. The most spectacular photographs usually come when high clouds reflect the entire red/yellow color range, and contrast with the blues and purples of the sky.

But how to catch that elusive moment?

It's late afternoon. The clouds are scattered above me in soft layers. I suspect tonight's sunset will be a show-stopper. A little after six o'clock, I begin driving around looking for subject matter to frame what is quickly becoming a brilliant display of color. I spot something, jump out of the car, set up the camera, and wait.

As the colors deepen and sweep further and further across the sky, I begin to shoot. With each frame I think, Surely it can't get more glorious than this! But over and over, the color blossoms a bit more and I just keep shooting. The sun at last disappears; and for another hour, a rich glow of crimson and deep lavender remains breathtakingly beautiful.

My stomach growls. I look at my watch. Nine o'clock! Deborah's long since had dinner on the table. I pack up and head home; late again, but content.

Lake Truxtun

Part of the water recharging program, Lake Truxtun is now a welcomed addition to the Kern River Parkway.

ALLEN ROAD

An October sunset is so intense, it resembles fire in the sky.

MOJAVE
For early risers, sunrise can provide nearly the same photographic opportunities as sunset, only in reverse.

Lake Isabella
In late autumn, the reservoir recedes, as runoff from the high country diminishes.

Bakersfield
Morning frost transforms blades of grass into green crystal.

WINTER

Winter is a realization that the temperate days of autumn are gone. You wake up to an ice-covered windshield, or a fog-shrouded landscape dotted with the silhouettes of dormant deciduous trees. On special days, the frost glistens on your lawn like a sparkling blanket of diamonds. You can look out your window in the morning and think that it's snowed!

In Kern County, winter is defined by the infamous fog. Tule fog, to be exact. It appears as a dense, impenetrable cloud cover that rises up from the Central Valley floor.

Now, most visitors say California is warm in winter, but our bone-chilling tule fog will put an overcoat on an out-of-towner faster than you can say "Jack Daniels." It makes winter a paradox in Kern County. It can be warmer in the mountains and colder in the valley, or warmer at night than during the day.

Through the camera's eye, winter is mysterious; a time when stark shapes melt into an atmosphere of whites and grays. The drama of fall fades into more subtle landscapes with cooler colors. Transitions are slow; golds turn to browns, blues to grays, reds to magenta.

But that's only part of the picture. From the rains of autumn and the insulating blanket of the fog, an Irish scene is created in the foothills. New green grasses mix with the golden hues of last year's growth to form a tapestry of immeasurable beauty.

Higher up, snowfall periodically buries the craggy peaks of the southern Sierra and dusts the foothills in soft white. Looking down from the mountains, you can swear the valley has become an ocean disappearing into a shroud of fog.

Shirley Meadows, Greenhorn
A break in a Sierra snowstorm creates an opening in the cloud cover.

MOUNT PINOS AREA
The morning sun glistens through ice crystals.

From top:

a. TEHACHAPI
Windmills peek through the cloud cover.

b. TEHACHAPI
Apple orchard windbreaks become lost in a fog of low clouds.

c. LAKE ISABELLA
Winter's chill settles over the reservoir.

Mojave

A lone Joshua tree stands tall through a high desert snowstorm.

Above: a. WALKER PASS
Joshua trees shiver on the eastern slope of the Sierra.

Left: b. WILLOW SPRINGS ROAD
Scrub brush glows red near Oak Creek, creating an eerie winter scene.

Above: *a.* NEAR GLENNVILLE
The Greenhorn Mountains rise above oak-filled ranges.

Right: *b.* CALIENTE-ARVIN ROAD
Dormant majestic oaks escape the valley fog.

Tower Line Road

Navel oranges ripening in the sun, with a snow-covered Bear Mountain in the background, create the ideal California postcard.

Near Woody
Oak trees are reflected
in a cattle watering pond.

Bakersfield
The sun glistens through droplets on a rain soaked willow tree.

Opposite page, clockwise from top left:

a. **Above Caliente**
Fingers of fog in the foothills

b. **Bakersfield**
Backwash sediment, water purification plant

c. **Hart Flat**
Clouds gather around mountain tops

d. **Buttonwillow**
Rainbow over plowed furrows

Bakersfield
Early morning fog rises from the river.

Above: *a.* KEENE
Black Mountain receives its first snow of the season.

Right: *b.* WHITE WOLF VALLEY
Dry-farming in the valley creates an ever-pleasing relief from Highway 58.

GRANITE STATION
Lichen paint boulders as foothills turn green from winter moisture.

KERN CANYON

Centuries of erosion
expose granite walls.
The first wildflowers appear
and before you know it,
winter becomes spring.
And so goes the cycle,
full circle.

Porterville Highway
These wooden derricks were dismantled a few years ago. The last remaining two are at opposite ends of Taft.

Opposite page:

Tehachapi
Ridge top windmills

THE HUMAN ELEMENT

How bizarre that a nature book should contain photos of constructed objects. Yet, I've found some of the most intriguing subject matter to be the play between the natural world and the world we've built for ourselves.

The lines separating these two worlds come together and interweave when I view them through the camera: The black lines of an oil derrick set against the bold colors of a sunset. The pattern the wind leaves upon a pile of gypsum. The perspective and depth created by a fence cutting through a meadow. The wooden planks of a desert cabin weathered with age. Shapes, colors and textures contrast, blend and enhance.

They emerge as objects of art.

Clockwise from top left:

a. TEHACHAPI
Fence

b. RANDSBURG
Cabin

c. KETTLEMAN HILLS
Windmill

d. BUTTONWILLOW
Power lines

e. HOLLOWAY ROAD
Gypsum

Oil derricks, pumping units and refineries are opportunities for me to photographically play with the surreal and the abstract.

It's true that the oil fields of Kern County create a wealth of riches for our economy. They are also a wealth of subject matter for those willing to view them with the eye of an artist.

Clockwise from top left: *a.* McKITTRICK *Pump unit*
b. TAFT *Derrick* *c.* BAKERSFIELD *Refinery*

Kern River Parkway Project

Every community dream brought to life owes its existence to a dedicated few. The Kern River Parkway Project is no exception. In 1980, a group of citizens came together to give form to an idea that had been floating around for years: To develop the Kern River in a way that would protect its ecosystem, yet make it accessible to the public.

An ad-hoc committee was created and initial corporate funding secured. A plan was drawn, detailing a park that would run alongside the river for over 30 miles, from the mouth of the Kern Canyon to Buena Vista Lake. Riparian land was both bestowed and purchased, and rehabilitation began.

Public support continued to grow. In 1995, the Kern River Parkway Foundation was established as a not-for-profit 501(c)(3) organization.

Today, around 20 miles of parkway exists. It includes bike and equestrian trails, rests points, bridges and river access areas. More than 4,000 trees, 200 shrubs and 4.5 acres of native grass and wildflower meadows have been planted to restore and re-vegetate the river's secondary flood plains.

Profits from *Buena Vista II* are benefiting the Kern River Parkway Foundation, and its mandate to preserve the beauty of the river and advance our understanding of it.

After Words

The worlds of photography are infinite. Flying above Kern County, you view a world of patterns and textures. Come down to the ground and get in a car; the world reformulates itself. You now start to see mid-range details — rivers, trees, lakes, ever-changing panoramas. Leave the car and head out on foot; the world again changes, becoming increasingly personal. Stop and kneel, and a whole other world opens up: a more explicit world of — what else? — patterns and textures.

My first book of scenic views, *Buena Vista*, was published in 1975. It represented five years of weekend trips throughout Kern County. Each image was coupled with a haiku verse written by my beloved friend, poet and naturalist, Ardis Walker.

It's now 20 years and thousands of exposures later. A lot of changes have taken place. Ardis and Gayle Walker have passed away. So has my father, Dr. Mortimer Iger. Some of my favorite views have been commercially developed, while others have changed naturally.

Most of my Kern County landscapes were photographed on special day trips to a specific location; others were taken while on the way to someplace else. I try to keep one of my cameras with me at all times, whether it be the 35mm Canon or Minolta, the $2^{1}/_{4}$ Bronica or Mamiya, or the 4x5 Calumet. All but a few locations were within one hour of Bakersfield. I haven't noted f-stop and shutter speed information except where it is useful in describing an unusual technique. Exposure details will be different when you are there.

I hope this book invites you to venture out and explore the diversity of Kern County. With or without camera, no matter the time of year, the many worlds of this place wait to be discovered.

Gregory Iger